Poems of Inspiration and Faith

Edited By William Roetzheim

Level 4 Press, Inc.
ISBN: 978-1-933769-45-5

Contents

Inspiration

Robert Burns

Epitaph on William Muir

An honest man here lies at rest
As e'er God with his image blest;
The friend of man, the friend of truth,
The friend of age, and guide of youth:
Few hearts like his, with virtue warmed,
Few heads with knowledge so informed:
If there's another world, he lives in bliss;
If there is none, he made the best of this.

Emily Dickinson

Hope is the thing with feathers

"Hope" is the thing with feathers—
That perches in the soul—
And sings the tune without the words—
And never stops—at all—
And sweetest—in the Gale—is heard—
And sore must be the storm—
That could abash the little Bird
That kept so many warm—

I've heard it in the chillest land—
And on the strangest Sea—

Yet, never, in Extremity,
It asked a crumb—of Me.

I'm nobody! Who are you?

I'm Nobody! Who are you?
Are you—Nobody—too?
Then there's a pair of us?
Don't tell! They'd advertise—you know!

How dreary—to be—Somebody!
How public—like a Frog—
To tell one's name—the livelong June—
To an admiring Bog!

The Props Assist the House

The Props assist the House
Until the House is built
And then the Props withdraw
And adequate, erect,
The House support itself
And cease to recollect
The Auger and the Carpenter—
Just such a retrospect
Hath the perfected Life—
A past of Plank and Nail
And slowness—then the Scaffolds drop
Affirming it a Soul.

Robert Frost

On a Tree Fallen Across the Road

The tree the tempest with a crash of wood
Throws down in front of us is not to bar
Our passage to our journey's end for good,
But just to ask us who we think we are

Insisting always on our own way so.
She likes to halt us in our runner tracks,
And make us get down in a foot of snow
Debating what to do without an ax.

And yet she knows obstruction is in vain:
We will not be put off the final goal
We have it hidden in us to attain,
Not though we have to seize earth by the pole

And, tired of aimless circling in one place,
Steer straight off after something into space.

Nancy Gustafson

Her Way to Soil

She imagined herself enduring,
A seed protected within a tough shell
Worthy to be womb and cradle,
Smooth, round, brown, hard
    A buckeye in God's pocket

But she drifted like a cottonwood seed,
A willy-nilly wind slafe without
A milestone chart or destination,
Her seedpod a white silk parachute
    Yet she found her way to soil.

One day a cocklebur in a big hurry
To catch a passing dog, pierced
Her parachute. They spiraled down entwined
And for a time both thrived, until
Beneath her green leaves deep shade arrived
Where grass can't grow for long
    And withers.

3

And she endured, sunk deep roots
Embraced the sky with spreading branches
And birthed a million seeds,
Drifting white silk parachutes.
　　　She had become all she imagined.

William Ernest Henley

Invictus

Out of the night that covers me,
Black as the pit from pole to pole,
I thank whatever gods may be
For my unconquerable soul.

In the fell clutch of circumstance
I have not winced nor cried aloud.
Under the bludgeonings of chance
My head is bloody, but unbowed.

Beyond this place of wrath and tears
Looms but the Horror of the shade,
And yet the menace of the years
Finds, and shall find, me unafraid.

It matters not how strait the gate,
How charged with punishments the scroll,
I am the master of my fate:
I am the captain of my soul.

Oliver Wendell Holmes

Sun and Shadow

As I look from the isle, o'er its billows of green,
To the billows of foam-crested blue,
Yon bark, that afar in the distance is seen,

Half dreaming, my eyes will pursue:
Now dark in the shadow, she scatters the spray
As the chaff in the stroke of the flail;
Now white as the sea-gull, she flies on her way,
The sun gleaming bright on her sail.

Yet her pilot is thinking of dangers to shun,—
Of breakers that whiten and roar;
How little he cares, if in shadow or sun
They see him who gaze from the shore!
He looks to the beacon
That looms from the reef,
To the rock that is under his lee,
As he drifts on the blast,
Like a wind-wafted leaf,
O'er the gulfs of the desolate sea.

Thus drifting afar to the dim-vaulted caves
Where life and its ventures are laid,
The dreamers who gaze
While we battle the waves
May see us in sunshine or shade;
Yet true to our course,
Though the shadows grow dark,
We'll trim our broad sail as before,
And stand by the rudder that governs the bark,
Nor ask how we look from the shore!

Marianne Moore

I May, I Might, I Must

If you will tell me why the fen
Appears impassable, I then
Will tell you why I think that I
Can get across it if I try.

Walt Whitman

Darest Thou Now O Soul

Darest thou now O soul,
Walk out with me toward the unknown region,
Where neither ground is for the feet
Nor any path to follow?

No map there, nor guide,
Nor voice sounding, nor touch of human hand,
Nor face with blooming flesh, nor lips,
Nor eyes, are in that land.

I know it not O soul,
Nor dost thou, all is a blank before us,
All waits undreamed of in that region,
That inaccessible land.

Till when the ties loosen,
All but the ties eternal, Time and Space,
Nor darkness, gravitation, sense,
Nor any bounds bounding us.

Then we burst forth, we float,
In Time and Space O soul, prepared for them,
Equal, equipped at last, (O joy! O fruit of all!)
Them to fulfill O soul.

Ella Wheeler Wilcox

Solitude

Laugh, and the world laughs with you;
Weep, and you weep alone.
For the sad old earth must borrow it's mirth,
But has trouble enough of it's own.

Sing, and the hills will answer;
Sigh, it is lost on the air.
The echoes bound to a joyful sound,
But shrink from voicing care.

Rejoice, and men will seek you;
Grieve, and they turn and go.
They want full measure of all your pleasure,
But they do not need your woe.
Be glad, and your friends are many;
Be sad, and you lose them all.
There are none to decline your nectared wine,
But alone you must drink life's gall.

Feast, and your halls are crowded;
Fast, and the world goes by.
Succeed and give, and it helps you live,
But no man can help you die.
There is room in the halls of pleasure
For a long and lordly train,
But one by one we must all file on
Through the narrow aisles of pain.

Rudyard Kipling

If

If you can keep your head when all about you
Are losing theirs and blaming it on you;
If you can trust yourself
When all men doubt you,
But make allowance for their doubting too;
If you can wait and not be tired by waiting,
Or, being lied about, don't deal in lies,
Or, being hated, don't give way to hating,
And yet don't look too good, nor talk too wise;

If you can dream—
And not make dreams your master;
If you can think—
And not make thoughts your aim;
If you can meet with triumph and disaster
And treat those two imposters just the same;
If you can bear to hear the truth you've spoken
Twisted by knaves to make a trap for fools,
Or watch the things
    you gave your life to broken,
And stoop and build 'em up
    with worn out tools;

If you can make one heap of all your winnings
And risk it on one turn of pitch-and-toss,
And lose, and start again at your beginnings
And never breath a word about your loss;
If you can force your heart and nerve and sinew
To serve your turn long after they are gone,
And so hold on when there is nothing in you
Except the Will which says to them: "Hold on!";

If you can talk with crowds
    and keep your virtue,
Or walk with kings—
    nor lose the common touch;
If neither foes nor loving friends can hurt you;
If all men count with you, but none too much;
If you can fill the unforgiving minute
With sixty seconds' worth of distance run—
Yours is the Earth and everything that's in it,
And—which is more—you'll be a Man my son!

Western Religion

Anonymous

The Anvil—God's Word

Last eve I passed beside a blacksmith's door
And heard the anvil ring the vesper chime;
Then, looking in, I saw upon the floor
Old hammers, worn with beating years of time.
"How many anvils have you had," said I,
"To wear and batter all these hammers so?"
"Just one," said he,
And then with twinkling eye,
"The anvil wears the hammers out, you know."

And so, thought I, the anvil of God's Word,
For ages skeptics blows have beat upon;
Yet, though the noise of falling blows
Was heard,
The anvil is unharmed—the hammers gone.

Gene Auprey

Hell (descending)

Well, it's hot, but not from brimstone's rage;
The burn is more akin to want. There's thirst,
If one can call it that, to slake the need
Of being known. The crush of souls, another
Myth, they're here but never reach to touch;
Demons too, from time to time, they pass
Like a wisp of scent: flowers you cannot find.
The presence of eternity is something else
That isn't here. You try, but cannot speak
Your name; it's gone and left you. Where?

William Cullen Bryant

To a Waterfowl

Whither, 'midst falling dew,
While glow the heavens with the last steps of day,
Far, through their rosy depths, dost thou pursue
Thy solitary way?

Vainly the fowler's eye
Might mark thy distant flight to do thee wrong,
As, darkly painted on the crimson sky,
Thy figure floats along.

Seek'st thou the plashy brink
Of weedy lake, or marge of river wide,
Or where the rocking billows rise and sink
On the chafed ocean side?

There is a Power whose care
Teaches thy way along that pathless coast,—
The desert and illimitable air,—
Lone wandering, but not lost.

All day thy wings have fann'd
At that far height, the cold thin atmosphere:
Yet stoop not, weary, to the welcome land,
Though the dark night is near.

And soon that toil shall end,
Soon shalt thou find a summer home, and rest,
And scream among thy fellows; reed shall bend
Soon o'er thy sheltered nest.

Thou'rt gone, the abyss of heaven
Hath swallowed up thy form; yet, on my heart
Deeply hath sunk the lesson thou hast given,

10

And shall not soon depart.

He, who, from zone to zone,
Guides through the boundless sky thy certain flight,
In the long way that I must tread alone,
Will lead my steps aright.

William Elliott

Still Life

It is fitting that three felons are nailed
Against the far wall of the sky, frozen
In the posture of the cruciform;

Fitting that the weary morning world
Should witness the end of a schism
On a hill, slowly; that the taciturn

Sky should collapse in a fragment of fog,
Dropping the impenetrable dregs
Of indifference on the mock-heroics.

Why do mirrors crack and goblets sting?
There holy by the grace of God he hangs.
The morning is meant for hysterics.

The Garden of Now

I have seen God sigh a monsoon,
Slip from the rim of a light-year
To rapids of stars, and dangle
His feet in the tumble and wake,
And withdraw them dripping the dross
Of fossils of ice turning lake.

I have seen God muscle the strings
Of orbit into mutiny

With a terse baton of lightning;
Heard the eardrum of creation
Burst, plunged in a font of eclipse;
And seen the house of heaven rise
With Author on their crater lips.

I have seen a tattered creature's
Starfish flesh sliced up at wit's end
Into the paradox of life.
I have seen God strike flint on flint
And spark the tinder of spirit
Raging with a yield of light.

I have walked in the Garden of Now
And found it as In the Beginning.

Ralph Waldo Emerson

The Rhodora
On being asked, Whence is the flower?

In May, when sea-winds pierced our solitudes,
I found the fresh Rhodora in the woods,
Spreading its leafless blooms in a damp nook,
To please the desert and the sluggish brook.
The purple petals, fallen in the pool,
Made the black water with their beauty gay;
Here might the red-bird come his plumes to cool,
And court the flower that cheapens his array.
Rhodora! If the sages ask thee why
This charm is wasted on the earth and sky,
Tell them, dear, that if eyes were made for seeing,
Then Beauty is its own excuse for being:
Why thou wert there, O rival of the rose!
I never thought to ask, I never knew:
But, in my simple ignorance, suppose
The self-same Power that brought me there
Brought you.

Kevin Hart

A Silver Crucifix on My Desk

Each day you wait for me,
Your arms
Raised as if to dive into my element,
Your bowed, precise body
Broken into the ways of earth. Someone
Has shrunk you
To a child's doll that I might understand
All that it is to be a man:
A simple cross
Where two worlds meet, a man
Caught there
And punished by the storm between two worlds,
A sword thrust into my desk
That tells me
With each new morning that the world
Will not escape
The world that we have made.
By evening
I no longer look your way,k but watch
Your shadow
Steal toward my hand, I hear you talk
In the clock's dialect
And my pen
Becomes an ancient nail. How often
Have I turned from you,
How often
Have I tried to shrink you down
And wear you round my neck,
As safe
As any of the stars you made.
You stand
Amongst the things of this world,
Old letters, photos,

13

An ashtray and a wallet, the things
That come and go, but you
I cannot move.

Extract from: Lightning Words

Prayer,
That terrible, strange thing—
A soul
Unclenching something fierce to play
Hide-and-go-seek,
Or taking the first step, again,
Into a boat without oars
With evening falling fast,
Or leaping
From a cliff, no one around,
And hoping to be gripped
Halfway down

Jerusalem

This is where the deserts end.
This is the city where the dead still live.
Here, at evening,
The sun and moon are both still full,
And when you arrive
The road can take you nowhere else.
Enter this inn
And see its empty table, its dead fire,
This window where
Those distant mountains stare into the past.

Remember
That woman with a broken jar,
That young man
Feeding swine in the sad desert twilight.

They say that silence leads us here,
That we are led
As if by hand, wind running fingers through the dust;
Inside, the silence
Will take you by the hand.
Here you bow to enter doors;
Here, a man once came
As one of us
To speak of all that we are not.

Now feel this stillness
Where two opposing forces clasp: this is the room
Where bread is broken
To make us whole, the inn of our desire.

The Last Day

When the last day comes
A ploughman in Europe will look over his shoulder
And see the hard furrows of earth
Finally behind him, he will watch his shadow
Run back into his spine.

It will be morning
For the first time, and the long night
Will be seen for what it is,
A black flag trembling in the sunlight.
On the last day

Our stories will be rewritten
Each from the end,
And each will end the same;
You will hear the fields and rivers clap
And under the trees

Old bones
Will cover themselves with flesh;
Spears, bullets, will pluck themselves

From wounds already healed,
Women will clasp their sons as men

And men will look
Into their palms and find them empty;
There will be time
For us to say the right things at last,
To look into our enemy's face

And see ourselves,
Forgiven now,
Before the books flower in flames,
The mirrors return our faces,
And everything is stripped from us,
Even our names.

The Yellow Christ

Gauguin

1.
Here, with milkmaids at his feet,
Not far from a row of blue houses,
A man as yellow as the sun,

A man but not a man,
Although he carried a shadow like ours,
Although his face was lined like ours;

Here, in the centre of a field
Enclosed by hedges, already abandoned
By women and a man

Who must return
To a world that they can understand,
The Cross holds him a little above the world.

2.
I know the distance between us
More than I know you, and you
Only as a darkness

That draws me like my own sleep;
Yet there can be no rest
With us forever apart, and I

Recoil into myself, I try to get by alone—
But see you always:
A face in the crowd,
The curve between two hills,

And feel dead. And so
I try again, knowing
No reason why you should come half-way

But you do,
Here, in Brittany, in a simple field,
The sky heavy with rain,
The apple trees in blossom.

Robert Hedin

At the Blessing of the children in Lourdes, Winter Solstice

They never imagined it would be like this—
The gurneys suddenly slipping away,
The braces all unclasping like hands.
And then the wading out, arm in arm,
Into the waters, the ghostly flowering
Of the night clothes. And for a moment
You can see them, out in the long columns
Of light, turning like white pinsheels
In the rain, the night so cold there's just
Their breath starting its long climb

Into the sky. And scattered there
In the smoke, the crutches shining
Like wingbones, the empty fleets
Of wheelchairs all overturned,
Their wheels spinning on their starlit hubs.

Gerald Locklin

Cathedral

We walk there from the opera house,
The Disney Philharmonic Hall,
The stages for the standard repertory
And experimental dramas,
The museum of contemporary art,
The expensive condos and bistros.

John Fante's Bunker Hill
Has not been flattened
Though he wouldn't recognize it.
You tread a gentle Golgotha
To enter the cathedral,
Descend the aisle to a broad,
Multi-angled,
Postmodernistically de-centered
(Or multi-centered)
Sanctuary,

Christ on a chicken-wire cross.

The altar flat as a table,
A mesa,
A place to share the masa,
The first communion or last supper.
"Superstition" is not sneered at.
The spiritual is not supercilious.
The devotions of the people—
To the virgin mother,

18

To Cesar Chavez,
Are celebrated in the slanting alcoves.
It must be the cathedral
Most invested with the turns of the imagination
Since Cordova
Or Coventry.

From outside,
A seeming fortress;
From within,
A window onto everywhere.
Enclave and refuge,
In and out of the city,
A part of it and yet
Apart from it.
The polyphonic music
Of the garden
Mixes waterfall and freeway traffic.
A Matterhorn
Of brown construction dirt
Is visible above the wall,
A ridge away.

A reredos from Spain,
Brought to the New World,
Carried north,
Stored
Then restored
To its former grandeur,
Finds its new home
In our Old World/New Aztlan.
Down the hill lie Chinatown,
Cinco de mayo,
Skid row,
Little Tokyo,
City hall, the courts, the cops,
The Biltmore and the Bradbury building,
The towers of the Bonaventure,

The convention
Center, coliseum,
Lakers, flatlands ghettos, harbors,
And the sea.

Just to the north,
The polyglot Chavez ravine,
Just to the east,
The "contagious" country hospital,
Just to the west:
Hollywood.
And on three sides of the city,
The mountains;
Beyond the mountains,
The vast Mojave desert;
To the west,
The sea,
Micronesia,
Asia.

The cynics mock
The cathedral
As "the Taj Mahony,"
After the cardinal who commissioned it.
I laugh,
But pin my hopes upon it
As a place of peace.
I want
To hear the echoes in it of "O Holy Night."
I hope
The devil in us doesn't blow it up.
And as for its inclusiveness,
A scrap of scripture is inscribed
On stone
In many languages;

And as for gender,
Well,

We've had for centuries
Our patron saint of tomboys:
Joan of Arc
(And now Joan of Arcadia).
Hart Crane shuddered
Like a bell tower into elegy.
Wallace Stevens knew the steeple
Was the pinnacle alike of ethics and aesthetics.

Auden sent petitions up,
Embraced the ambiguities of light and power,
Came to know, with age,
Anxiety.
The rich can still buy their way in
(To crypt-interment, anyway),
But the poor of heart shall still see god,
Inherit the cathedral
And the kingdom that will be
Or not be
Of this earth.

Henry Wadsworth Longfellow

The Three Silences of Molinos
To John Greenleaf Whittier

Three Silences there are: the first of speech,
The second of desire, the third of thought;
This is the lore a Spanish monk, distraught
With dreams and visions, was the first to teach.
These Silences, commingling each with each,
Made up the perfect Silence, that he sought
And prayed for, and wherein at times he caught
Mysterious sounds from realms beyond our reach.
O thou, whose daily life anticipates
The life to come, and in whose thought and word
The spiritual world preponderates.
Hermit of Amesbury! Thou too hast heard

Voices and melodies from beyond the gates,
And speakest only when thy soul is stirred!

Susan Marie

Pieta

I have always envied Michelangelo.

Not that I have met him
But in my mind's eye,
I see David
Standing

In all his glory.
His pectorals and abdominals
Intact
And Mother Mary
Cradling her son
Frozen in time
An ice princess.
No one ever noticing
The woman
And the crows feet
That hide beside her eyes.

Krista Nielsen

Prayer

The others around me laugh
But I do not hear them
For there is nothing worth hearing
Except the sound
Of my mind connecting
With you.

Coventry Patmore

The Toys

My little Son, who look'd from thoughtful eyes
And moved and spoke in quiet grown-up wise,
Having my law the seventh time disobey'd,
I struck him, and dismiss'd
With hard words and unkiss'd,
—his Mother, who was patient, being dead.
Then, fearing lest his grief should hinder sleep,
I visited his bed,
But found him slumbering deep,
With darken'd eyelids, and their lashes yet
From his late sobbing wet.
And I, with moan,
Kissing away his tears, left others of my own;
For, on a table drawn beside his head,
He had put, within his reach,
A box of counters and a red-vein'd stone,
A piece of glass abraded by the beach,
And six or seven shells,
A bottle with bluebells,
And two French copper coins,
Ranged there with careful art,
To comfort his sad heart.
So when that night I pray'd
To God, I wept, and said:
Ah, when at last we lie with trancèd breath,
Not vexing Thee in death,
And Thou rememberest of what toys
We made our joys,
How weakly understood
Thy great commanded good,
Then, fatherly not less
Than I whom Thou hast molded from the clay,
Thou'lt leave Thy wrath, and say,
'I will be sorry for their childishness.'

Brian Roberson

The Light and The Skies

Follow the light into the world,
Harsh light upon your eyes.
Look first to the faces,
Then out into the skies.

Tamra Trevino

An Amazing Tale

By chance, I heard an amazing tale
Of perfect love that was not for sale
From God's only Son, who would come one day
Gather His people and take them away
I long for what they're talking about
And pray, believing without a doubt.

Me

Jesus be Jesus in me
No longer me but Thee
Jesus be Jesus in me
So me can be the me meant to be

John Greenleaf Whittier

By their Works

Call him not heretic whose works attest
His faith in goodness by no creed confessed.
Whatever in love's name is truly done
To free the bound and lift the fallen one
Is done to Christ. Whoso in deed and word

Is not against Him labors for our Lord.
When He, who, sad and weary, longing sore
For love's sweet service, sought the sisters' door,
One saw the heavenly, one the human guest,
But who shall say which loved the Master best?

Trust

The same old baffling questions! O my friend,
I cannot answer them. In vain I send
My soul into the dark, where never burn
The lamps of science, nor the natural light
Of Reason's sun and stars! I cannot learn
Their great and solemn meanings, nor discern
The awful secrets of the eyes which turn
Evermore on us through the day and night
With silent challenge and a dumb demand,
Proffering the riddles of the dread unknown,
Like the calm Sphinxes, with their eyes of stone,
Questioning the centuries from their veils of sand!
I have no answer for myself or thee,
Save that I learned beside my mother's knee;
"All is of God that is, and is to be;
And God is good." Let this suffice us still,
Resting in childlike trust upon His will
Who moves to His great ends unthwarted by the ill.

Troy Wilson

The Lord's Dance

He spoke, they heard,
He showed, they saw,
He led, they followed;
A conga line was born.

William Wordsworth

We are Seven

A simple child,
That lightly draws its breath,
And feels its life in every limb,
What should it know of death?

I met a little cottage girl:
She was eight years old she said;
Her hair was thick with many a curl
That clustered round her head.

She had a rustic, woodland air,
And she was wildly clad:
Her eyes were fair, and very fair;
—her beauty made me glad.

"Sisters and brothers, little Maid,
How many may you be?"
"How many? Seven in all," she said
And wondering looked at me.

"And where are they? I pray you tell."
She answered, "Seven are we;
And two of us at Conway dwell,
And two are gone to sea.

"Two of us in the church-yard lie,
My sister and my brother;
And, in the church-yard cottage, I
Dwell near them with my mother."

"You say that two at Conway dwell,
And two are gone to sea,
Yet ye are seven! I pray you tell,
Sweet Maid, how this may be."

Then did the little Maid reply,
"Seven boys and girls are we;
Two of us in the church-yard lie,
Beneath the church-yard tree."

"You run about, my little Maid,
Your limbs they are alive;
If two are in the church-yard laid,
Then ye are only five."

"Their graves are green, they may be seen,"
The little Maid replied,
"twelve steps or more from my mother's door,
And they are side by side.

"My stockings there I often knit,
My kerchief there I hem;
And there upon the ground I sit,
And sing a song to them.

"And often after sunset, Sir,
When it is light and fair,
I take my little porringer,
And eat my supper there.

"The first that died was sister Jane;
In bed she moaning lay,
Till God released her of her pain;
And then she went away.

"So in the church-yard she was laid;
And, when the grass was dry,
Together round her grave we played,
My brother John and I.

"And when the ground was white with snow,
And I could run and slide,

My brother John was forced to go,
And he lies by her side."

"How many are you, then," said I,
"if they two are in heaven?"
Quick was the little Maid's reply,
"O Master, we are seven."

"But they are dead; those two are dead!
Their spirits are in heaven!"
'T was throwing words away; for still
The little Maid would have her will,
And said, "Nay, we are seven!"

Eastern Religion

Maroula Blades

Mandala

I choreograph myself to the situation,
Creating maps of inner and outer worlds,
Pentagrams, circles, compact shapes,
Houses of pure air for the mind to breathe in.
No cages.
Freethinkers
And the morally bankrupt are welcome.
No painful extractions from the mind.
I softly go behind, touching the deepness,
The unknown factor
Where demons flee the details, the yellow fog.
Meditative art.
Like a battery
I work off the positive and the negative,
Every shade
Holds a secret that is pivotal to life.
A dominion of ages,
A universe,
Listening to dark and light tones,
Easing down the slave lake of life.
I brush away cobwebs
From the corners of thoughts,
Stored in cryogenic rooms
At the base of memory.
Wade in my maternal peace,
Paint the joys and the pains,
Use the spaces in my sphere;
Make my body pregnant with colour.
Let the colours bleed,
It's my wish,
As every tint is vast and beautiful,

Every line infinite,
Climbing frames,
Leading upwards and outwards.
Where I exist,
Freedom has a place to grow,
Free of a hunched back
To flow brightly back to the source, the light.

William Blake

To See a World in a Grain of Sand

To see a world in a grain of sand
And a heaven in a wild flower,
Hold infinity in the palm of your hand
And eternity in an hour.

Londis Carpenter

Why I Write

I Write So You'll Remember
That the Wizard of Oz
And the Wizard of Ur Are the same.
And I am "the man with the hammer"
You call Thor!
I Write So You'll Remember when
Gods walked the earth side by side with men.
I Write So You'll Remember
Walking with me through the garden
Hand in hand.

The walls of earth are littered
With the ruins of fallen stars
And runes of men.
The Circles of Grain
And the Wheels of Sky are real.

Moses' cloud has now become
Ezekiel's wheel.

Two million gods and twenty thousand sects; And
looking into space I see my face
And god and I are one.

William Elliott

Nothingness

For Kiyomi)

Standing amid the pebbles of his mind,
He looked outside
And saw the leaves
Strewn in approximate precision;
But he declined
To stay inside.

Standing in a heap of leaves,
He looked, stood back,
And looked;
And then went back inside
And found the pebbles of his mind
Already raked.

Sitting by the pebbles,
He rose and raked them over
In concentric ovals in approximate precision;
Stood back and looked,
And declined to go outside
To rake the leaves.

Theatrical Etiquette

Any more than you would
Five nashi

In a wicker basket

Or the basket empty

You come to No
Prepared not
To applaud gods.

Nancy R. Hatch

The Answers Lie Within

Look deep, the answers lie within
We reach the beginning . . . In the end

Gerald Locklin

David Hockney: *My Father, Paris,* Jan. 1974 And *The Artist's Mother,* 1972

I'm no Buddhist,
But it seems to me that people over there,
At least that generation,
Realized better than people here,
That contentment lay in enjoying
What they had,
Rather than coveting what they didn't.

The grass was green enough
In their own front yards,
If they (or their neighbors)
Were lucky enough to have a front yard.

And I also suspect
The fat guy would have taught,

"If you must paint the world,
Which is already the creation
Of a greater artist than yourself,
Paint those around you,
And the places where you find yourself,

And the spirit will show through
If and when
It feels like it."

What Ornette Coleman Teaches

Our freedom
Must become the freedom of the jazz man,
Not of the man who seeks through jazz to re-imagine,
Satisfy,
Modify
And enhance
The freedom of the listener,
Which is not a freedom.

If your freedom is willing
To become this other freedom,
Which is not the modification
Of what already exists,
Of melody, harmony, and rhythm,

But the freedom which no longer
Knows the categories of analysis
But which is the freedom of not-thinking,
The freedom of the instinct of the moment,
The freedom of movement
Through an uncharted,
Unmapped, unlearned territory,

Then you will on your deathbed
Understand the freedom of his music,
Of my words,

The freedom of unsituated improvisation,
Improvisation
Without context, history,
Or filing for the future,

Not a riff, but a futureless gesture,

The metafreedom that cannot exist,
That can only exist,
That is,
Under the auspices of its unthinkability.

Pagan Religion

Emily Dickinson

I taste a liquor never brewed

I taste a liquor never brewed—
From Tankards scooped in Pearl—
Not all the Vats upon the Rhine
Yield such an Alcohol!

Inebriate of Air—am I—
And Debauchee of Dew—
Reeling—thro endless summer days—
From inns of Molten Blue—

When "Landlords" turn the drunken Bee
Out of the Foxglove's door—
When Butterflies—renounce their "drams"—
I shall but drink the more!

Till Seraphs swing their snowy Hats—
And Saints—to windows run—
To see the little Tippler
Leaning against the—Sun—

William Roetzheim

Fertility Doll

Returning home I brought my wife some gifts,
among them was a carved figure—an ugly
woman with huge breasts and bigger belly.
Hawaiians said her name was Hi'iaka.

She stood beside our bed and watched, her eyes
reflecting red in candlelight, her shadow
dancing with obscene and naked joy
to hear *Bolero* by Ravel, to hear
the primitive music of need and want.
And in one month my wife told me that she
was pregnant after trying for so long.

We loaned her out to Loni, who was pregnant
that same month. And then the breathless call
when Hi'iaka had the same results
for Betty Lou, after four years of trying,
crying, clinics too. But now my laughing
wasn't easy, now I found that I
was queasy when I thought of Hi'iaka's
naked dancing, watching with those eyes
that seemed to glow.

I know, I know she's just
a doll and not a god, not like my god,
the western god that toppled her and all
her kind two hundred years ago, although
she dances on our wall, her shadow leaps
and falls, and quietly she plants her seeds
of pagan thought, of faith in ancient gods.

William Butler Yeats

The Indian upon God

I passed along the water's edge below the humid trees,
My spirit rocked in evening light,
The rushes round my knees,
My spirit rocked in sleep and sighs;
And saw the moor-fowl pace
All dripping on a grassy slope,
And saw them cease to chase
Each other round in circles,
 and heard the eldest speak:
Who holds the world between His bill
And made us strong or weak
Is an undying moorfowl, and He lives beyond the sky.
The rains are from His dripping wing,
The moonbeams from His eye.
I passed a little further on and heard a lotus talk:
Who made the world and ruleth it,
He hangeth on a stalk,
For I am in His image made, and all this tinkling tide
Is but a sliding drop of rain between His petals wide.
A little way within the gloom a roebuck raised his eyes
Brimful of starlight, and he said:
The Stamper of the Skies,
He is a gentle roebuck; for how else, I pray, could He
Conceive a thing so sad and soft,
 a gentle thing like me?
I passed a little further on and heard a peacock say:
Who made the grass and made the worms
And made my feathers gay,
He is a monstrous peacock,
 and He waveth all the night
His languid tail above us, lit with myriad spots of light.

Questioning Religion

Richard Archer

Changing Viewpoints

Over the years my faith has crumbled,
Eroded by a lifetime of disillusion.
And there behind its once strong front,
I found my atheism hiding.

And now as I watch my atheism erode,
Piece by piece it is worn down by time.
And as it is chipped and falls away,
I wonder what will be exposed beneath?

Charles Baudelaire

From Fuses I - On God

Even if God did not exist,
Religion would still be holy and divine,
God is the only being who, in order to rule,
Does not need even to exist.
Creations of the mind
Are more alive than matter.

William Blake

The Tiger

Tiger! Tiger! Burning bright,
In the forests of the night,
What immortal hand or eye
Could frame thy fearful symmetry?

In what distant deeps or skies
Burnt the fire of thine eyes?
On what wings dare he aspire?
What the hand dare seize the fire?

And what shoulder, and what art,
Could twist the sinews of thy heart?
And when thy heart began to beat,
What dread hand? And what dread feet?

What the hammer? What the chain?
In what furnace was thy brain?
What the anvil? What dread grasp
Dare its deadly terrors clasp?

When the stars threw down their spears,
And watered heaven with their tears,
Did he smile his work to see?
Did he who made the Lamb make thee?

Tiger! Tiger! Burning bright
In the forests of the night,
What immortal hand or eye
Dare frame thy fearful symmetry?

David Coulon

God Save Me From Your Followers!

Lord of my life,
You pipe a dirge,
They hear a jig.
They sing they didn't,
I dance they did.

William Elliott

The Fortunate Fall

Only the serpent's hiss was in the hush
As single-filing through the brush
They abandoned the given way
Freely, although indeed evicted by
The landlord in the clay;

Slunk like hoodlums from their tapered garden,
Thinking that he had forbidden
The act that they had committed.
But him they were driven and directed by,
Not merely permitted.

The scowl they mistook for his displeasure,
And the loud language as a measure
Of the moment of their one wrong,
Were relief. Peeved and pleased,
He conjectured why
They had taken so long.

Thomas Hardy

The oxen

Christmas Eve, and twelve of the clock.
'Now they are all on their knees,'
An elder said as we sat in a flock
By the embers in hearthside ease.

We pictured the meek mild creatures where
They dwelt in their strawy pen,
Nor did it occur to one of us there
To doubt they were kneeling then.

So fair a fancy few would weave
In these years! Yet, I feel,
If someone said on Christmas Eve,
'Come; see the oxen kneel,

'In the lonely barton by yonder coomb
Our childhood used to know,'
I should go with him in the gloom,
Hoping it might be so.

Gerard Manley Hopkins

Carrion Comfort

Not, I'll not, carrion comfort,
Despair, not feast on thee;
Not untwist—slack they may be—
These last strands of man
In me ór, most weary, cry I can no more. I can;
Can something, hope, wish day come,
Not choose not to be.

But ah, but O thou terrible,
Why wouldst thou rude on me
Thy wring-world right foot rock?
Lay a lion limb against me? Scan
With darksome devouring eyes
My bruisèd bones? And fan,
O in turns of tempest, me heaped there;
Me frantic to avoid thee
    And flee?

Why? That my chaff might fly;
My grain lie, sheer and clear.
Nay in all that toil, that coil,
Since (seems) I kissed the rod,
Hand rather, my heart lo! Lapped strength,
Stole joy, would laugh, chéer.
Cheer whom though? The hero
Whose heaven-handling flung me,
    Fóot tród
Me? Or me that fought him?
O which one? Is it each one? That night,
    That year
Of now done darkness I wretch
Lay wrestling with (my God!) My God.

Gerald Locklin

The Moneychangers In the Temple Were a Good Start

It may very well be,
As Hollywood would have it,

The Greatest Story Ever Told,

But I would have preferred it if,

Just for dramatic effect,

43

Just for the satisfaction of the hubris
And the nemesis
(A nd not writing off the possibility
Of Aronold Schwarzenegger's
Recreating the role),

Christ had ridden fewer asses
And kicked more.

John Milton

On His Blindness

When I consider how my light is spent
Ere half my days in this dark world and wide,
And that one talent which is death to hide,
Lodged with me useless, though my soul more bent
To serve therewith my Maker, and present
My true account, lest He returning chide,
'Doth God exact day labor, light denied?'
I fondly ask. But Patience to prevent
That murmur, soon replies, 'God doth not need
Either man's work or his own gifts. Who best
Bear his mild yoke, they serve him best.
His state
Is kingly: thousands at his bidding speed,
And post o'er land and ocean without rest;
They also serve who only stand and wait.'

E. Louise Osburn

To My Atheistic Friend

If you are right and I am wrong
And Christ was just a man,
When we die, it won't much matter
But I hope you understand
If I am right and you are wrong,

When this earth's reduced to rubble
And the devil welcomes you to Hell
You're in a heap of trouble.

William Roetzheim

Christ's Face Found in Photos from Mars

The headline answered questions seldom posed
In supermarkets. Why was Christ no longer
Close to me? Why had our dialogue
Become a monologue, then silence, deep
As altar candles snuffed, their curling smoke
Like question marks?

Perhaps he's gone to Mars
To rest from saving sheeplike souls on Earth.
It seems unfair that he should go away
And leave me here, although I must admit
That even God His father had a day
Of rest. At least I know just where he's gone.

Faith
(From the sonnet ring—Seven Heavenly Virtues)

While in the snowy woods I think what might
Have been. I lost my faith at seventeen,
That is, that godly faith in wrong and right,
In or out. I live somewhere between,
A world of doubt where falling snow makes ugly
Bright, and covers beauty with its cold.
I'd dig below, but what's beneath lies snugly
Waiting for rebirth. I am consoled
With icy gems on lonely walks, at least
I say I am. At home I roll a trail
To god from a ten dollar bill, released

From snorted snow that laughs as I inhale.
    In Africa this bill would help, it's true—
    Two children fed and educated too.

Jim Denison

The auctioneer's gavel banged, I'd saved
The storage shed contents. Salvation sales
Occupied my time, but, Christ, what junk.
A testament to people's hopeless faith
In resurrected fashions, born again
Belongings, sin of waste avoided. Home
I carted cardboard boxes,
Sorted through the trash:
Worn clothes and broken toys, chipped plates,
A family Bible, and old papers baptized
With the stain of seeping rain—a mount
Of trash. That night I sat by firelight,
Sipped wine, and read
Those molded pages, poems
Penned in scrawling hand by Denison.
Some were good, and some were bad,
But each portrayed
A bitter man and thankless world.
As pages turned a shape appeared,
Not clear and sharp
But faded . . . Dark. Jim Denison
Was sitting there. I understood, or thought
I did, and said that
Writing poems gave him immortality.
He shook his head,
Looked 'cross the room
To stare at old belongings,
Then blinked. He said
"You must read and believe."
I watched him fade, remained confused,
And later
Woke to realize it must have been

A dream. I tossed the clothes and toys,
The plates
And poems,
Hesitated with the Bible,
I don't know why,
And then tossed that as well.

Faith

Emily Bronte

I am the Only Being Whose Doom

I am the only being whose doom
No tongue would ask no eye would mourn
I never caused a thought of gloom
A smile of joy since I was born

In secret pleasure—secret tears
This changeful life has slipped away
As friendless after eighteen years
As lone as on my natal day

There have been times I cannot hide
There have been times when this was drear
When my sad soul forgot its pride
And longed for one to love me here

But those were in the early glow
Of feelings since subdued by care
And they have died so long ago
I hardly now believe they were

First melted off the hope of youth
Then Fancy's rainbow fast withdrew
And then experience told me truth
In mortal bosoms never grew

'Twas grief enough to think mankind
All hollow servile insincere
But worse to trust to my own mind
And find the same corruption there

Thomas Campion

Integer Vitae

The man of life upright,
Whose guiltless heart is free
From all dishonest deeds,
Or thought of vanity;

The man whose silent days
In harmless joys are spent,
Whom hopes cannot delude,
Nor sorrow discontent;

That man needs neither towers
Nor armor for defense,
Nor secret vaults to fly
From thunder's violence:

He only can behold
With unaffrighted eyes
The horrors of the deep
And terrors of the skies.

Thus, scorning all the cares
That fate or fortune brings,
He makes the heaven his book,
His wisdom heavenly things;

Good thoughts his only friends,
His wealth a well-spent age,

The earth his sober inn
And quiet pilgrimage.

Emily Dickinson

I had been hungry all the years

I had been hungry, all the Years—
My Noon had Come—to dine—
I trembling drew the Table near—
And touched the Curious Wine—

'Twas this on Tables I had seen—
When turning, hungry, Home
I looked in Windows, for the Wealth
I could not hope—for Mine—

I did not know the ample Bread—
'Twas so unlike the Crumb
The Birds and I, had often shared
In Nature's—Dining Room—

The Plenty hurt me—'twas so new—
Myself felt ill—and odd—
As Berry—of a Mountain Bush—
Transplanted—to a Road—

Nor was I hungry—so I found
That Hunger—was a way
Of Persons outside Windows—
The Entering—takes away—

Edgar Lee Masters

Aner Clute

Over and over they used to ask me,
While buying the wine or the beer,
In Peoria first, and later in Chicago,
Denver, Frisco, New York, wherever I lived,
How I happened to lead the life,
And what was the start of it.
Well, I told them a silk dress,
And a promise of marriage from a rich man—
(It was Lucius Atherton).
But that was not really it at all.
Suppose a boy steals an apple
From the tray at the grocery store,
And they all begin to call him a thief,
The editor, minister, judge, and all the people—
"A thief," "a thief," "a thief," wherever he goes.
And he can't get work, and he can't get bread
Without stealing it, why, the boy will steal.
It's the way the people
Regard the theft of the apple
That makes the boy what he is.

Marianne Moore

Injudicious Gardening

If yellow betokens infidelity,
I am an infidel.
I could not bear a yellow rose ill will
Because books said that yellow boded ill,
White promised well.

However, your particular possession,
The sense of privacy,

Indeed might deprecate
Offended ears, and need not tolerate
Effrontery.

.

.

WE BOOK ™

What is WEbook?

WEbook.com is an online community where writers, readers, and "feedbackers" create great books and cast their votes to make their favorite undiscovered writers the next published authors.

WEbook is an innovative avenue for new writers to find an audience, satisfying the dreams of millions of aspiring authors and tapping the wisdom of the crowd to create a unique new form of creative work: community-sourced books.

Level 4 Press teamed up with WEbook to find fresh new poets for five anthologies: Poems of Inspiration and Faith; Poems of Ghosts, Evil, and Superstition; Poems of Nature; Poems of Romance; and Modern Nursery Rhymes. WEbookers submitted their best work, read each other's poems, and gave each other feedback. A total of 57 poems written on WEbook—most by brand new, previously unpublished poets—are included in Level 4 anthologies.

WEbook.com is a whole new way of looking at how books are written and picked for publication. Learn more and see how you can be part of the revolution at www.WEbook.com.